THE MOST Disgusting ANIMALS ON THE PLANET

BY JOHN PERRITANO

CAPSTONE PRESS
a capstone imprint

Velocity is published by Capstone Press,
1710 Roe Crest Drive, North Mankato, Minnesota 56003.
www.capstonepub.com

 Books published by Capstone Press are manufactured with paper
containing at least 10 percent post-consumer waste.

Perritano, John.
   The most disgusting animals on the planet / by John Perritano.
      p. cm.
(Velocity. disgusting stuff.)
   Includes bibliographical references and index.
   Summary: "Discusses animals that have disgusting characteristics and behaviors"—Provided
by publisher.
   ISBN 978-1-4296-7535-2 (library binding)
1. Curiosities and wonders—Juvenile literature. 2. Animal behavior—Miscellanea—Juvenile
literature. 3. Aversion—Miscellanea—Juvenile literature. I. Title. II. Series.
AG243.P367 2012
   591.5—dc23   2011029240

Editor: Barbara Linde
Project Manager: Archna Bisht
Art Director: Suzan Kadribasic
Designers: Ankita Sharma, Joita Das, Manish Kumar, Ravinder Kumar
Image Researchers: Akansha Srivastava, Saloni Vaid

Photo Credits
AP Images: LM Otero/Associated Press, 25; Corbis: Anup Shah/Terra, 6-7, Dr. Richard Kessel & Dr. Gene
Shih/Visuals Unlimited, 44 (top), Ken Lucas/Visuals Unlimited, 42-43, Steve Austin, 26-27, Visuals Unlimited/
Encyclopedia, 32-33 (bottom), Wolfgang Kaehler, 10-11; FLPA: W T Miller, 14-15; Getty Images: Jeff
Rotman/The Image Bank, 28-29; iStockphoto: Ifish, 20-21; NHPA: Mark Bowler, 37 (top); Nick Richter, 23;
Photolibrary: Friedemann Koster/Oxford Scientific (OSF), 4-5, Tui De Roy/Oxford Scientific (OSF), 35;
Science Photo Library: Jamesh. Robinson, 44-45, Maryann Frazier, 36-37, Rondi & Tani Church, cover, 33,
Volker Steger, 38-39 ; Shutterstock: Chris Fourie, 31, EcoPrint, 41, Efendy, 8-9, Geoffrey Kuchera, 18-19,
Hubskaya Volha, 12-13 (top), 34, kurt G, 16-17, PhotoBeard, 14 (bottom), 15 (top), Photo market, 38,
P.schwarz, title page, 12-13, Villiers Steyn, 40; Thinkstock: Hemera, 22, iStockphoto, 9, 30-31

Printed in the United States of America in Stevens Point, Wisconsin.
102011   006404WZS12

Table of Contents

GROSS - OUT ANIMALS

We all have nasty habits. We pass gas. We burp. We spit. Some of us pick our noses and a few even wipe ear wax on our clothes!

But nothing compares to what goes on in the animal kingdom. Many animals are cute and cuddly. A few are downright adorable—until you get to know them. The vampire finch seems like a beautiful bird, until it lands on the back of another animal and sucks its blood. Skunks make lovable cartoon characters, but you don't want a skunk to get close enough to spray you.

Some animals wouldn't live very long if they weren't disgusting. They use nauseating tricks to stay alive. The zorilla sprays a nasty, smelly, gagging jet of liquid when it is in danger. Animals also have to eat—and quite often they eat each other!

Let's go on safari to learn about some of the most stomach-turning animals on the planet. Take a deep breath first—some of these animals might make you gag, and a few might even make you sick!

Chapter 1

NAUSEATING EATERS

You don't want these animals sitting next to you at the dinner table!

Field of Screams

When jackals are feeling threatened, they let out an eerie, shrill scream. They also make yipping sounds to call their young. To us, all jackals sound the same. But each baby jackal knows when its parents are calling. They ignore the call of other adult jackals and only head home when they hear their parents call.

Picky Eaters

Jackals are in the dog family and are no bigger than Labrador retrievers. But you definitely won't want one as a pet. Jackals are scavengers.

Sometimes these carnivores find their own food, but they prefer to wait until other animals, such as lions and tigers, are done eating what they have killed. When those animals leave, the jackals creep up and gobble up the leftovers.

Jackals aren't fussy. They don't care how long the carcass has been sitting in the hot sun. They don't care that the animal's flesh is crawling with maggots. It's not that jackals are lazy. They actively hunt antelopes and gazelles. They have no problem attacking a sheep if one strolls by. Still, jackals don't think twice about chowing down on what's already dead. For them it's fast food.

Before jackals are old enough to scavenge, they have a disgusting eating habit. Baby jackals lap up food that their parents have vomited. And it gets worse. If the young pups are full, the adults don't let a good thing go to waste. They'll eat what they just threw up!

Jackals wait while the hyena finishes its meal. Then they will move in for the leftovers.

scavenger—an animal that feeds on animals that are already dead
carnivore—an animal that eats only meat
carcass—the body of a dead animal

Poop Eaters

If there is tasty **dung** on the ground, the dung beetle can't be far behind.

dung—solid waste from animals

Dung beetles have been living on Earth for more than 50 million years. Most dung beetles seem to especially enjoy the poop of plant-eating **herbivores**.

Dung beetles get **nutrients** from the **digested** plants in the poop. Animal poop is also full of water.

There are thousands of **species** of dung beetles. They fall into one of three groups: rollers, tunnelers, and dwellers.

- **Rollers** mold dung into tiny balls, just as you mold a piece of clay. The beetles roll the poop balls away and bury them. They later return to lay eggs on the buried poop.

- **Tunnelers** bury dung in underground tunnels so they can feast on it later.

- **Dwellers** build their homes inside dung piles.

herbivore—an animal that eats only plants
nutrient—a substance needed by a living thing to stay healthy
digest—to break down food so it can be used by the body
species—a group of animals with similar features

Flesh-eating Dragons

Dragons don't just hang out in fairy tales. A real-life dragon makes its home in Indonesia. Its name is the komodo dragon. This reptile will eat almost anything in sight.

There are between 3,000 and 5,000 komodo dragons living in the wild. These rare beasts are scavengers, but they also hunt live animals for their supper. Whether it's a cow or a water buffalo, no one likes to mess with a komodo dragon. Here's why.

The dragon sits and waits before grabbing hold of its victim. With its razor-sharp teeth, the lizard tears into its prey. Still, the animal doesn't die right away. Instead, the dragon's teeth open large wounds. These wounds are then flooded with deadly **venom**. The venom reduces the prey's blood pressure. The animal goes into shock and slowly bleeds to death. Then it is chow time.

Dirty Mouth

Scientists used to think that the saliva of komodo dragons was deadly. Inside the dragon's mouth lurk 50 different types of bacteria. But scientists have now learned that venom produced by glands inside the komodo's mouth is the real killer.

venom—a poisonous liquid produced by some animals
saliva—the clear liquid in the mouth of a person or animal that helps with swallowing and digestion
bacteria—very small living things that exist all around you and inside you; some bacteria cause disease
gland—an organ in the body that makes natural chemicals or helps substances leave the body

Hungry Hyenas

In the movie *The Lion King*, hyenas are villains. In real life, they are pretty wicked too.

Although they might look like large dogs, hyenas belong to the same class of animals as cats. Hyenas hunt in packs. They chase down giraffes and other slow-moving animals.

Spotted hyenas celebrate the kill by giggling. This slight laugh tells other hyenas that it's dinner time. Hyenas are not fussy. They eat every bit of their victims. They use their sharp teeth to rip their prey apart. They eat skin, muscles, and even bones. Hyenas gorge themselves by eating as much as 40 pounds (18 kilograms) of food in one sitting.

FACT

The ancient Egyptians tried to tame hyenas and also raised them for food.

Chapter 2

SICKLY SPRAYERS

Snarls and growls aren't the only behaviors that keep away a predator. Spraying an enemy with disgusting fluid is a way for some animals to protect themselves.

Smelly Polecats

With their black and white bodies and cute faces, many people think striped polecats are adorable! Keep your distance, though. Some people think that the spray from these animals smells worse than the spray from skunks!

predator—an animal or plant that hunts other animals for food

Although they look like small skunks, zorillas are part of the weasel family. They eat mice, frogs, bugs, and lizards. They sleep in rock crevices during the day and hunt at night. Other animals steer clear of the striped polecat. Why? It is one of the smelliest animals on the planet.

The zorilla uses its foul scent to keep predators away. Scent glands are inside the polecat's body. These glands spew a disgusting fluid when a polecat feels threatened.

Luckily for its enemies, spraying is the last thing a zorilla does if it is in danger. A zorilla will first raise the hair on its back and lift its tail to make itself look larger. If the attacker doesn't run away, the polecat shoots a fluid that hurts its enemy's eyes. Finally, it will let out the nasty smelling spray.

Toxic Beetles

Tight shoes can cause skin to blister. Did you know that stepping on a beetle can cause skin to blister too?

Blister beetles are long, narrow, plant-loving insects. The blister beetle contains a poisonous chemical called cantharidin. The beetles use the poison to avoid being eaten. When a predator, such as a spider, attacks the beetle, the poison gets on the spider's skin. The skin burns and blisters. Ouch! The spider stops its attack.

Blister beetles can also harm much larger animals, like horses. The beetles often burrow in the hay in barns. If a horse eats a lot of beetles while chomping on hay, the horse can get sick and die.

FACT

Doctors sometimes use cantharidin to remove warts from a person's skin.

Stinky Skunks

Pepé Le Pew might be a cute cartoon character, but he smells. "When you are a skunk," he says, "you learn how to hold your breath for a long time."

Skunks are known for their foul smell. Spraying is the skunk's last line of defense. When a skunk senses danger, it will first growl and hiss, and then angrily pound its paws. If the attacker doesn't get the message, it will turn its back to its victim. Then the skunk will lift its tail and fire away. The horrible smell drives predators away. The spray is not poisonous, though. It won't harm a person or animal. But it will make them smell bad for a long time.

FACT

A skunk's spray is an oily mixture of several sulfur compounds. Glands under the skunk's tail produce the liquid, which smells like rotten eggs. The spray can travel more than 10 feet (3 meters).

compound—a substance made of two or more elements bonded together

Chapter 3

DISGUSTING DEFENDERS

It's a dog-eat-dog world in the animal kingdom. That's why animals have to be disgusting to survive.

sea cucumber threads

Sea of Gunk

When a sea cucumber feels threatened, predators better beware!

Sea cucumbers got their name because they are shaped like cucumbers. But unlike the tasty green vegetable, sea cucumbers have soft bodies and tough, slippery skin. This helps them squeeze into crevices and even liquefy themselves to hide from predators.

When an enemy comes near, some sea cucumbers squeeze out sticky spaghetti-like threads. The web of thread traps the predator, and the sea cucumber escapes.

Instead of squeezing out sticky threads, a different type of sea cucumber spits out its organs. This creates a slimy gunk that traps the enemy long enough for the sea cucumber to paddle away. The organs of the sea cucumber grow back in a few weeks.

Another type of sea cucumber can turn itself into a greasy mush. It hides in small cracks in rocks. Once inside the crack, the sea cucumber hardens its skin so the predator can't get it. When the danger is gone, the sea cucumber gets mushy again and leaves the rock. Its body goes back to normal.

Poisonous Poop

Three-lined potato beetles are an attractive target for predators. That's because they do not have hard shells. But these little bugs have a nasty surprise when an enemy comes along—a shield of poop.

Bittersweet nightshade is a purple-flowered weed that has poisonous leaves. The three-lined potato beetle loves to eat nightshade. The poison doesn't hurt the beetle, but when the bug poops, its feces is poisonous.

Potato beetles pile the toxic poop on their backs for protection. Oncoming predators get a whiff of the poison poop and think twice about attacking. Can you blame them?

FACT

Many types of animals use the same method as the potato beetle to keep predators away. Scientists call this type of defense a "fecal shield."

Leapin' Lizards!

In the deserts of Mexico and the southwestern United States lives a lizard with an eye-popping way to beat back its enemies.

The horned lizard has a couple of useful ways of defending itself from predators like coyotes and **raptors**. It can blend into its surroundings by making its skin color lighter or darker. The lizard can also hide by flattening its body.

The lizard saves its gross defense for times when it feels really threatened. Tiny spaces in the eye sockets of the horned lizard fill with blood. As an attacker approaches, the lizard's blood pressure goes up. Splat! Out shoots a jet of blood. The blood can fly up to 7 feet (2.1 m) with amazing accuracy.

raptor—a bird of prey

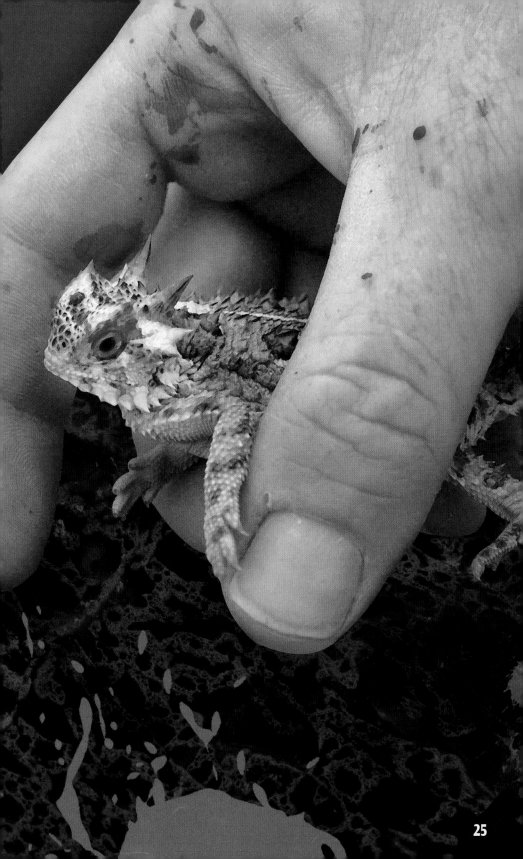

Freaky
Fulmars

There's nothing more adorable than a baby chick. However, fulmar chicks are far from adorable. Fulmar means "foul gull," and rightly so.

Fulmars are birds that live near the ocean. They build their nests high up on cliffs. When fulmar parents are not at home, other birds can swoop down and pick the chicks out of their nests. The babies know what to do. They vomit on their attackers. The fulmar's puke is a smelly, oily liquid created in the bird's **digestive system**.

If the oil sticks on the attacker's feathers, the predator can die. The oil makes it difficult for the birds to fly away. They can fall into the ocean and drown.

Fulmar chicks are not the only ones who vomit on attackers. Adult fulmars use this disgusting practice to defend themselves as well.

digestive system—the group of organs responsible for breaking down food into energy for the body and for getting rid of waste

Chapter 4

PUTRID PAIRS

It's not easy living in the wild. Not all animals can survive on their own. Some form a close and revolting partnership with other animals.

Awful Anglerfish

Many people would agree that the anglerfish is one of the ugliest animals in the ocean. And if the male anglerfish's appearance doesn't make it unappealing enough, its disgusting eating habit does.

There are more than 300 species of anglerfish. Most live in the Atlantic Ocean. They have big heads, sharp teeth, and spiny backs.

Female anglerfish have an efficient way of finding food. Hanging above the mouth of a female is a piece of **dorsal** spine. The female uses this piece of spine as a fishing rod. The "rod" is tipped with a piece of glowing flesh that other animals can't resist. Chomp! When a fish swims close to snap the glowing bait, the female anglerfish gobbles it up.

The male anglerfish does little for its food. To survive, the much smaller male latches onto the well-fed female. The male becomes a **parasite**. He bores through the female's skin and lives off her blood. Six or more males can latch onto a female at once.

FACT

Female anglerfish have mouths big enough to swallow prey much larger than themselves.

dorsal—located on the back
parasite—an animal or plant that lives on other animals or plants

Terrible Tahrs

It can be hard for animals to find mates. To make this job easier, some animals have unique ways of finding partners.

Sometimes what they do is revolting. This is the case for the tahr, a distant cousin to the goat.

Male tahrs don't spend much time with females throughout the year. However, during mating season, male tahrs compete for the attention of the females.

When the male finds a female he likes, he wants to know her better. The two play a game of tag. Sometimes the female walks away. She wants to find someone she likes better. However, when the female is interested in a male, she'll pee near him. The male takes the gross behavior as a sign that the female is attracted to him!

Want a Drink?

Many animals use urine to attract one another. Male giraffes actually taste the females' pee to see which one would make a good mate. Some monkeys pee into their hands and wash themselves in the urine. Scientists say a pee-covered male is attractive to the female.

Chapter 5

BLOOD SUCKERS

Legendary vampires aren't the only creatures that drink blood. Many animals need to drink the liquid to survive.

Lousy Lampreys

Sea lampreys used to live only in the Atlantic Ocean. In the 1800s, these eel-like fish found their way from the ocean into inland lakes and rivers. By the 1900s, they were considered a big problem.

Sea lampreys live off the blood of other fish. These creatures can grow to be more than 20 inches (51 centimeters) long. They attach their huge disk-like mouths to the side of their prey. Then they suck blood and other body fluids out of the fish. A lamprey will attach itself to a fish for days or even weeks. They can suck the life out of lake trout, salmon, and sturgeon.

The lamprey kills almost everything it latches onto. A single sea lamprey can kill 40 pounds (18 kg) of fish during its lifetime. The sea lamprey has wiped out many fish populations.

Deadly Mouth

The sea lamprey's mouth is a deadly weapon. It has a suction cup ringed with sharp teeth. After the lamprey attaches its mouth to a fish, its pointed teeth grab hold of its victim. The lamprey then uses its sharp tongue to pierce the fish's skin. The lamprey oozes a substance that keeps the wound open and the blood flowing. It swims away only after its stomach is full or the fish dies.

Blood-thirsty
Birds

Dracula would be right at home on the Galápagos Islands in the Pacific Ocean. That's where the vampire finch lives.

These feathery predators are not like typical backyard finches. The vampire finch feasts on more than seeds and bugs. It thrives on the blood of other birds!

The bird the vampire finch feasts on the most is called a booby. The vampire finch uses the booby as its own personal blood bank. A finch lands on the back of the seabird and pecks away. In no time, the booby starts to bleed. Blood oozes out of the wounds.

The vampire finch drinks the blood. Soon other finches arrive and start drinking too. While the wounds might look horrible, they do not do any lasting damage to the booby. Vampire finches can survive on the booby's blood during long periods of **drought**.

Egg Rolling

Although the vampire finch doesn't seem to harm an adult booby, the booby's eggs are always in danger. Vampire finches use their beaks to roll booby eggs off rock ledges. The eggs fall and break. The vampire finch then slurps up the developing chick.

drought—when the land is dry because of too little rain

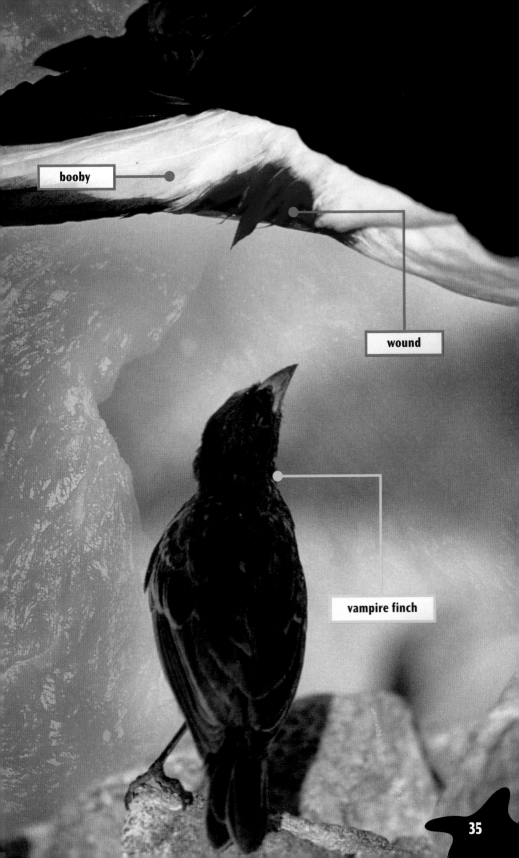

booby

wound

vampire finch

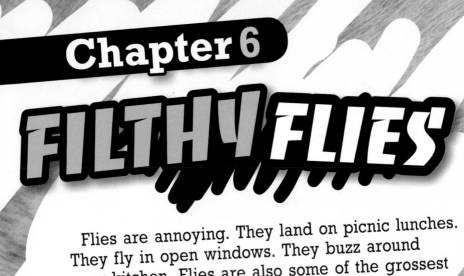

Chapter 6

FILTHY FLIES

Flies are annoying. They land on picnic lunches. They fly in open windows. They buzz around your kitchen. Flies are also some of the grossest bugs around.

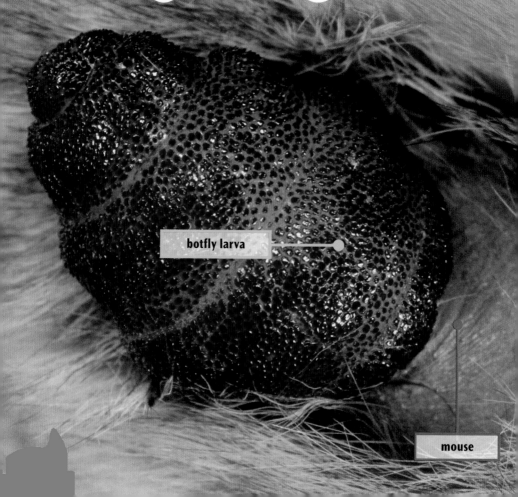

botfly larva

mouse

Skin Crawlers

Its name sounds like something out of an old horror movie. But the human botfly may be worse than any Hollywood monster.

Why is that? The human botfly is a parasite. It preys on humans and animals living in Central America, Mexico, and South America.

First, the female botfly lays its eggs on a mosquito or tick. When those bugs feed on a person or animal, the eggs hatch. The tiny larvae, or maggots, burrow under the skin where they live about 12 weeks. The maggots tunnel deep into the muscle. Tiny hooks hold the maggots in place. People who have had botfly eggs in them say they can feel the maggots crawl under their skin!

In about 30 days, the large maggots want to find a way out. They dig their way through the skin and poke their heads out. Eventually, the maggots fall to the ground and turn into adult flies.

Botflies on Animals

Different species of botflies prey on animals, including squirrels, rabbits, cattle, deer, horses, and sheep. Sometimes the botflies burrow into the animals as they do in humans. Other times, the animals eat the eggs along with hay or grass. The eggs develop into maggots inside the animals' stomachs. The maggots come out in the animals' dung.

larva—an insect at the stage of development between an egg and an adult

Flesh Eaters

Maggots are among the most repulsive creatures on the planet. Still, we can't get along without them.

Maggots play an important role in how living things **decompose**. When an animal dies, blowflies see a tasty meal. They land on the rotting carcass, where they drink blood and other body fluids. This gives the flies energy to mate. As they eat, the flies vomit. The vomit makes the food easier to digest. When the flies are full, they lay eggs on the rotting flesh. When the eggs hatch, maggots crawl out and continue to feed on the carcass. Maggots eventually turn into winged blowflies.

Doctors sometimes use blowfly maggots to treat infections. When other treatments haven't worked, doctors will put maggots on an open wound. Once on the person's skin, juices in the maggots' digestive systems dissolve the dead tissue around the wound. The nasty insects then eat the mushy mix, swallowing the bacteria that caused the infection.

decompose—to rot or break down

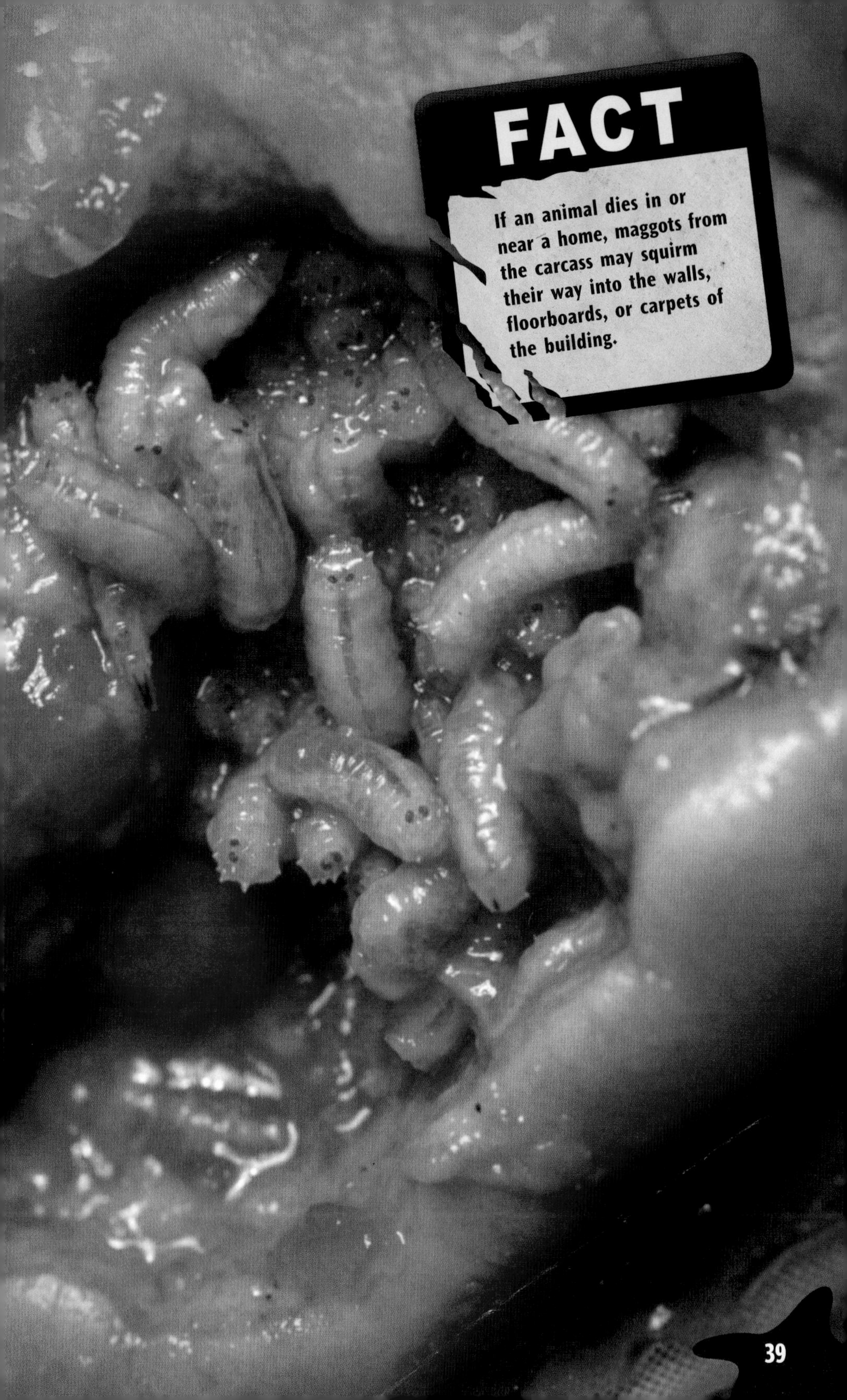

FACT

If an animal dies in or near a home, maggots from the carcass may squirm their way into the walls, floorboards, or carpets of the building.

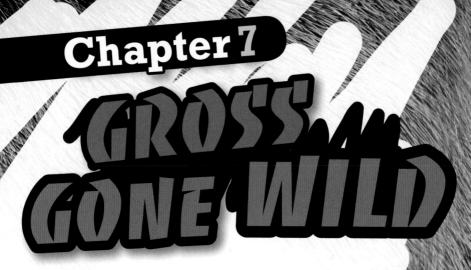

Chapter 7

GROSS GONE WILD

Being gross is natural for many animals. But some creatures take gross to a higher level than others.

Hitching a Ride

Large animals in Africa don't need to wear flea and tick collars. All they need is an oxpecker.

Oxpeckers are a type of bird. The oxpecker's nickname is "tickbird." That's because ticks are one of their favorite meals. Where there is a zebra, giraffe, or some other big animal, chances are a flock of oxpeckers aren't far behind. They land on the backs of these animals and eat ticks. The oxpecker also drinks blood from the wounds made by the tick.

But blood and ticks are not the only things oxpeckers eat. They also feast on lice, mites, and flies. They have even been known to chow down on the earwax and snot of animals!

oxpecker

Slime Eels

You would think that an animal with four hearts would have a heart when it comes to its neighbors.

Not the hagfish. It preys on worms, small fish, and other tiny creatures that live nearby. Hagfish look somewhat like sea lampreys. They are long and slimy. They have four hearts, but no jaws, eyes, or stomachs.

Hagfish have a disgusting way of eating. They attach themselves to other fish. Hagfish then tunnel themselves into the fish and eat the creatures from the inside out. They scrape off the meat with their pointed tongues and stuff it into their funnel-shaped mouths.

And their disgusting behaviors don't stop there. The hagfish is known as a "slime eel." When a predator swims by, the hagfish sneezes out slimy gunk. The slime contains tiny, thin strands called fibers that make the slime strong. The "superslime" can clog the gills of the attacker, killing the predator.

When the danger passes, the hagfish slips from its slimy cocoon. How does the fish do that? It ties itself in a knot. The fish then wiggles the knot all the way down its body. As the knot travels, it scrapes away the goo.

FACT

Hagfish are usually from 18 to 32 inches (46–81 cm) long. They come in a variety of colors, including pink, blue-gray, and brown. Some of them have black or white spots.

Tale of the Tapeworms

magnified view of a tapeworm head

If you have a dog, you might know that dogs can get tapeworms. But tapeworms can also live in the intestines of humans!

Humans get tapeworms by eating meat from an animal that is full of tapeworm eggs. When this happens, a tapeworm will begin to grow inside the intestines.

The bodies of most types of tapeworms are made up of many sections called segments. These segments join behind the tapeworm's head. Tapeworms feed on the food you digest. As they eat, they get longer. Since a tapeworm doesn't have a mouth, it absorbs food through its body.

intestine—a long tube that carries and digests food and stores waste products

tapeworm body

The Disgust Goes On

Hopefully you enjoyed your revolting trip through the animal kingdom. While some animals have good reasons to be gross, many do not. Dogs eat their own poop and vomit. Why? Because they can. Even humans do many disgusting things. How many can you name?

Glossary

bacteria (bak-TEER-ee-uh)—very small living things that exist all around you and inside you; some bacteria cause disease

carcass (KAHR-kuhs)—the body of a dead animal

carnivore (KAHR-nuh-vohr)—an animal that eats only meat

compound (KAHM-paund)—a substance made of two or more elements bonded together

decompose (dee-kuhm-POHZ)—to rot or break down

digest (dy-GEST)—to break down food so it can be used by the body

digestive system (dye-JESS-tiv SISS-tuhm)—the group of organs responsible for breaking down food into energy for the body and for getting rid of waste

dorsal (DOR-suhl)—located on the back

drought (DROUT)—when the land is dry because of too little rain

dung (DUHNG)—solid waste from animals

gland (GLAND)—an organ in the body that makes natural chemicals or helps substances leave the body

herbivore (HUR-buh-vor)—an animal that eats only plants

intestine (in-TESS-tin)—a long tube that carries and digests food and stores waste products

larva (LAR-vuh)—an insect at the stage of development between an egg and an adult

nutrient (NOO-tree-uhnt)—a substance needed by a living thing to stay healthy

parasite (PAR-uh-site)—an animal or plant that lives on other animals or plants

predator (PRED-uh-tur)—an animal that hunts other animals for food

raptor (RAP-tur)—a bird of prey

saliva (suh-LYE-vuh)—the clear liquid in the mouth

scavenger (SKAV-uhn-jer)—an animal that feeds on animals that are already dead

species (SPEE-sheez)—a group of animals with similar features

venom (VEN-uhm)—a poisonous liquid produced by some animals

Read More

Goldish, Meish. *Disgusting Hagfish.* Gross-Out Defenses. New York: Bearport Publishing, 2009.

Murray, Julie. *Disgusting Animals* That's Wild!: A Look at Animals. Edina, Minn.: ABDO Publishing, 2010.

Weakland, Mark. *Gut Bugs, Dust Mites, and Other Microorganisms You Can't Live Without.* Nasty (but Useful!) Science. Mankato, Minn.: Capstone Press, 2011.

Internet Sites

FactHound offers a safe, fun way to find Internet sites related to this book. All of the sites on FactHound have been researched by our staff.

Here's all you do:

Visit *www.facthound.com*

Type in this code: 9781429675352

Index